SOLITAIRE
BATTLESHIPS

108 Challenging
Logic Puzzles

PETER GORDON
& MIKE SHENK

Sterling Publishing Co., Inc.
New York

Thanks to Jaime Poniachik.

The six Battleship puzzles in the introduction originally appeared in *Games Magazine*, *Games World of Puzzles Magazine*, and *Games Premium Puzzles Magazine*. Reprinted by permission.

Designed by Peter Gordon.

Library of Congress Cataloging-in-Publication Data Available

10 9 8 7 6 5 4 3 2 1

Published by Sterling Publishing Company, Inc.
387 Park Avenue South, New York, N.Y. 10016
© 1998 by Peter Gordon & Mike Shenk
Distributed in Canada by Sterling Publishing
%o Canadian Manda Group, One Atlantic Avenue, Suite 105
Toronto, Ontario, Canada M6K 3E7
Distributed in Great Britain and Europe by Cassell PLC
Wellington House, 125 Strand, London WC2R 0BB, England
Distributed in Australia by Capricorn Link (Australia) Pty Ltd.
P.O. Box 6651, Baulkham Hills, Business Centre, NSW 2153, Australia

Sterling ISBN 0-8069-5956-8

CONTENTS

INTRODUCTION

Battleships puzzles are a solitaire version of the classic paper-and-pencil game of the same name. The object of each puzzle is to find the locations of the 10 ships in the fleet hidden in a section of ocean represented by the 10-by-10 grid. The fleet consists of one battleship (four grid squares in length), two cruisers (each three squares long), three destroyers (each two squares long), and four submarines (one square each).

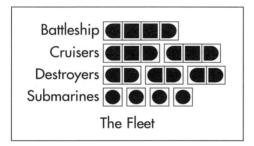

Battleship
Cruisers
Destroyers
Submarines

The Fleet

The ships may be oriented either horizontally or vertically in the grid, but no two ships will occupy adjacent grid squares, *even diagonally*. The digits along the side of and below the grid indicate the number of grid squares in the corresponding rows and columns that are occupied by vessels.

In nearly all Battleships puzzles, the contents of a few of the squares have been revealed to start you off. These "shots" come in four types:

Water This square contains no ship.

Submarine This square consists of a submarine, and thus must be surrounded by water.

End of a ship This square can be oriented in any of four directions. It indicates the end of either a destroyer, cruiser, or battleship. The square adjacent to the flat side must be occupied by a ship segment. All other surrounding squares are filled with water.

■ **Middle of a ship** This is either the middle segment of a cruiser, or one of the two middle segments of the battleship. Either it has the squares to the left and right occupied by ship segments and the ones above and below it empty *or* the squares above and below are occupied by ship segments and the ones to the left and right are empty. In both cases, the diagonally adjacent squares are filled with water. In fact, any time a square is occupied, all of the diagonally adjacent squares must have water in them, because ships can't touch diagonally.

The most basic strategy to Battleships solving has three parts:

1. Fill in what you know in squares adjacent to given ship segments.

2. Fill in water in rows and columns that have all of the ship segments already in place.

3. Fill in ship segments in rows and columns that must have all of their remaining empty spaces filled in order to equal the corresponding number.

For the simplest Battleships, this is all that is needed to solve the puzzle. Take a look at the puzzle in Figure 1. (On page 22 are larger versions of the six sample puzzles in this chapter for you to follow along on.)

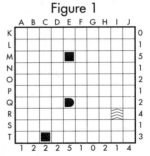

Figure 1

Throughout this chapter, columns of the grid will be referred to with uppercase letters A through J, while rows will be referred to with letters K through T. In this way, any square in the grid can be referenced with two letters: AK means the upper left square where column A crosses row K. In the example below, there are ship segments at CT, EM, and EQ, and water at IR.

To solve this puzzle, start with strategy 1: Fill in squares adjacent to the given ships. You know that the flat side of an end of a ship must have a ship segment next to it, so you can fill in DQ with a ship segment—it must be the other end of a destroyer because the row can only contain two ship segments.

You can then fill in the spaces surrounding the destroyer with water. The ship segment at CT must be the middle part of a cruiser or one of the middle sections of the battleship. The ship must be horizontal (if it were vertical, it would extend below the bottom edge of the grid), so the squares to the left and right of CT (BT and DT) must have ship segments in them. Since row T can only have a total of three ship segments in it, BT-CT-DT must be a cruiser. The squares surrounding it can be filled in with water. The filled-in square at EM is also the middle section of a cruiser or one of the middle sections of the battleship. You don't know which yet, but you know that the four squares that touch a ship segment diagonally must be water, because ships never touch diagonally. Keep this in mind at all times for easier solving. Your grid should now look like Figure 2.

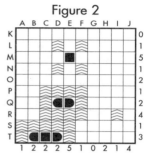

Figure 2

Now use strategy 2. Rows K, Q, and T, and columns D and G have all of their ship segments accounted for, so you can fill all the blank squares in those rows and columns with water. Your grid should now look like Figure 3.

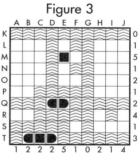

Figure 3

Now look at EM. It must be part of a ship that goes vertically because DM is water, and the ship can no longer extend to the left. You could have figured this out using strategy 3 instead, since column E has only three blank spaces, all of which need to be filled with ship segments to reach the five needed. Since four segments in a row in column E are filled, that must be the battleship. Row R also has to have all of its empty spaces filled with ship segments. The left part, AR-BR must be a destroyer. The right part, HR and JR, must have ship segments in them, too. Don't make the mistake of filling them in with submarines—although they may be submarines, each one could also be the top half of a destroyer. To indicate that it's filled in with an unidentified ship segment, use a small dot in the middle of the square. Your grid should now look like Figure 4.

Whenever you fill in a ship segment, go back to strategy 1. Here, you can put water in FM and FO, and IS, too, since it touches a ship segment diagonally. And using strategy 2, you can put water in what's left of columns A and B and rows L and N, to get Figure 5.

It's time to use strategy 3 again. Column F must have a submarine in that empty space (it can't be something bigger because it's surrounded by water), and row M must have all four of its empty spaces filled with ship segments, making a submarine on the left and a cruiser on the right. This gives you Figure 6.

When you return to strategy 1 this time, you'll find it doesn't help, but strategy 2 does: You can fill in the blank spaces of columns C, H, and I and row S with water, since they already contain the required number of ship segments. Your grid now looks like Figure 7.

The dots in row R are surrounded by water, so they must be submarines. And since you need two more ship segments in column J and have two spaces available, you can finish off the puzzle by filling those spaces with a destroyer. A quick double check verifies that you have all the required ships, so you're done (Figure 8).

The three basic strategies, though certainly important, will take you only so far. If you hope to regularly finish all but the easiest puzzles, you'll need more advanced strategies. When

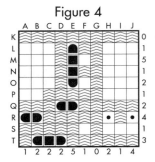

Figure 4

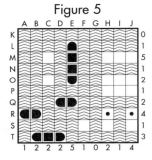

Figure 5

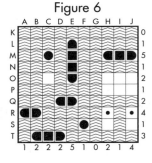

Figure 6

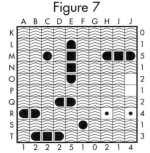

Figure 7

you've reached a point at which the basic strategies provide no further help, the simplest advanced strategy is to try placing the largest ship that hasn't yet been located. If you haven't found where the battleship goes, try finding a spot for it. If the battleship is already in place, then look for spots for the cruisers. Here's an example (Figure 9).

First, of course, you should fill in what you can using the basic strategies. Your grid should now look like Figure 10.

Now, consider where the battleship can go. It must go in a row or column that has a four or higher. Only two qualify: row L and column E. It can't fit in row L, though—that row already contains a ship that can't be the battleship since there's only room for it to be a cruiser or destroyer, and the battleship can't go in the right part of the row since then there would be more than four spaces filled by ships. So the battleship must go in column E. But where in the column? Its top can be at either EN, EO, EP, or EQ. You don't know which, but if you look at those four possibilities, you'll notice that in every case EQ is filled with a ship segment. So you can put a dot in EQ. Any time you put a dot in a square, you can immediately put water in the diagonally adjacent squares (since ships never touch diagonally), so fill in FP and FR with water. And look at row Q. It has its three ship segments, so the rest of it must be water—fill them in (Figure 11).

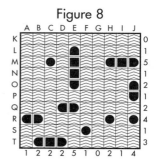

Figure 8

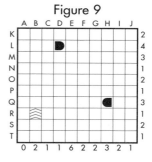

Figure 9

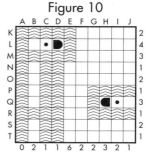

Figure 10

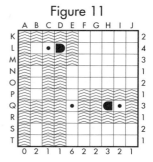

Figure 11

When you've filled in all the spaces surrounding a square that contains a dot, you can convert the dot to its proper ship segment. Here, square IQ must be the right end of a destroyer. Whenever you make a change using an advanced strategy, go back to you basic strategies to see if you can use them. Row R has only one empty space, and it has a one at the end of it, so that empty square must be filled with a ship segment. Since you don't yet know what type it is, put a dot in it. That dot gives you water in FS. Your grid should now look like Figure 12.

Now you'll need to think. Consider the four places the battleship can go. The first is EN-EO-EP-EQ. That's not possible because to put it there, ER would have to contain water, but it doesn't. The next possibility is EO-EP-EQ-ER. It fits, but putting it there would require water in EN and ES, leaving only one more blank space in column E, and two are needed to bring the total number of ship segments to six. So that possibility is out, too. The next possibility, EP-EQ-ER-ES, has the same problem—EO and ET would need to be water, leaving only one blank space (at EN), when two are needed to bring the total to six. So the last possibility, with the battleship at EQ-ER-ES-ET, must be correct; fill it in. That allows you to put water at EP and FT (Figure 13).

Now go back to the basic strategies. Fill in square BP with a dot (remember not to assume it's a submarine—it could extend upward!), and EN-EO with a destroyer. This puts water at FM, FN, and FO (Figure 14).

Continue using the basic strategies. Column F must contain a destroyer at FK-FL, and water

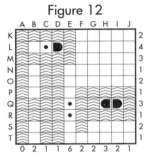

Figure 12

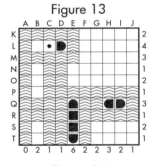

Figure 13

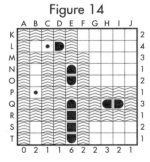

Figure 14

must go in GK, GL, and GM. Now look at row M. HM-IM-JM must be a cruiser. This puts water in HL, IL, JL, GN, HN, IN, and JN. You can also fill in BN, IK, IO, IS, IT, JK, JO, JS, JT, BT, GT, and HT with water, giving you Figure 15.

You can complete the puzzle with the basic strategies. Finish rows K and L first, and then columns B, G, and H. When you're done, your solution should look like Figure 16.

This example illustrates how a typical Battleships puzzle of medium difficulty can be solved. You start with the three basic strategies, then use some logical thinking to break through to the next step, and finish by again using the basic strategies. More difficult puzzles require more of these thought steps. Here's an example (Figure 17).

Using the basic strategies, you can get to the point shown in Figure 18.

Now try the advanced strategy of finding where the biggest remaining ship goes. In this case, the biggest ship not yet placed is the battleship. It can only go in column I (the only row or column with a four or higher), at either IK-IL-IM-IN or IL-IM-IN-IO. In both cases, IL, IM, and IN have ship segments in them, so you can fill those in. You can also put water in IT, since the battleship in the top of column I will use up all four allotted ship segments (Figure 19).

As always, after using an advanced strategy, you should reapply the basic strategies. You'll find you can put water in all the empty

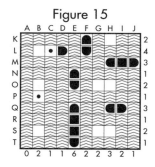

Figure 15

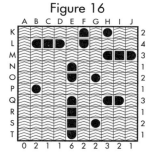

Figure 16

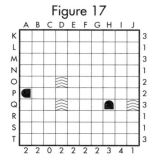

Figure 17

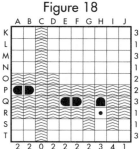

Figure 18

spaces of rows L and N, as well as in HK, HM, HO, JK, JM, and JO since they're diagonally adjacent to ship segments (Figure 20).

This is as far as the you'll get with the basic strategies. It's time to try advanced strategy again. You know roughly where the battleship goes (somewhere at the top of column I); consider now where the cruisers can go. Only rows and columns with a three or higher are possibilities. You can rule out column I (since the battleship accounts for all four segments there), row M (since, after the component of the battleship is taken into account, there are only two more ship segments in that row), and row Q (which already has its three ship segments). That leaves column H, row K, and row T as possibilities. Two of those three must contain cruisers. If a cruiser goes in row K, it can only fit in the center section of four consecutive white squares. No matter where a cruiser fits in those four squares, square FK will have a ship segment in it. Similarly, if a cruiser goes in row T, it can only fit in the center section of five consecutive white squares. No matter where it fits in those five squares, square FT will have a ship segment in it. Since column F already contains one ship segment (FQ), the two cruisers can't go in both rows K and T at the same time, or else column F would have one too many ship segments in it. So one of the cruisers must be located in column H (and the other in either row K or row T). Column H can have only three

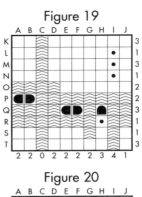

Figure 19

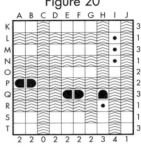

Figure 20

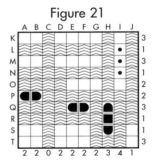

Figure 21

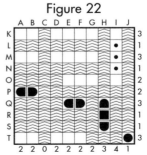

Figure 22

ship segments in it, so the cruiser must be a part of what's already there. Fill it in with the surrounding water (Figure 21).

Now back to the basic strategies. Fill in water in the remaining spaces of row S; then it's clear that JT is a submarine (Figure 22).

Bingo! You now know the cruiser can't go in row T, since there's already a submarine in it, leaving only two remaining ship segments. So the cruiser must be in row K. You don't know its exact location; there are two possibilities, but in either case EK and FK must contain ship segments, and AK, BK, and IK must contain water, since all three ship segments in that row will be used up by the cruiser (Figure 23).

Back to the basic strategies. The battleship location has been determined in column I. You can fill the empty spaces in columns E and F with water, making GO a submarine (Figure 24).

Basic strategies still haven't finished off the puzzle. So again, look for a place for the largest remaining ship. You need one more destroyer. Row K is out—it's reserved for the cruiser. There are only two places left on the board with two adjacent white spaces: AM-BM and AT-BT. If the ship went in AM-BM, then AT and BT would contain water, leaving row T with at most two ship segments in it, which isn't enough. So the destroyer must instead be at AT-BT (Figure 25).

And now, at last, you can finish the puzzle with the basic strategies (Figure 26).

Figure 23

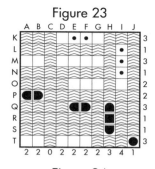

Figure 24

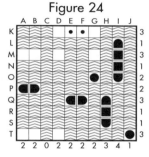

Figure 25

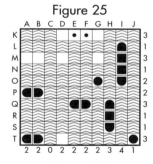

Figure 26

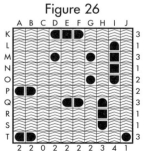

By now, you should know enough to get through all but the toughest of Battleships puzzles. Further advancement requires practice and more advanced strategies. Take a look at the next puzzle (Figure 27).

After using the basic strategies, the puzzle should look like Figure 28.

The biggest ship not yet placed is the battleship. Where can it go? Plenty of places: It could fit in one place in row N, one place in column B, or in any of four places in column J. You probably don't want to try that many possibilities. It's time for a different strategy: Look around the board for rows and columns that are almost determined. In particular, look for rows and columns in which the number of ship segments left to place is one less than the number of empty spaces. In this puzzle, row N needs four ship segments and has only five empty spaces. Row O needs three ship segments in the four remaining empty spaces. You'll find a similar condition in row Q, but for this puzzle you should concentrate on rows N and O. Consider square CN. If it's filled with a ship segment, then both BO and DO would have to contain water (since they're diagonally adjacent to CN). But that would leave only two empty spaces in row O for three ship segments—an impossibility! So CN can't contain a ship segment; fill it in with water. After filling CN with water, the basic strategies will take you a long way (Figure 29).

Now you go back to the first advanced strat-

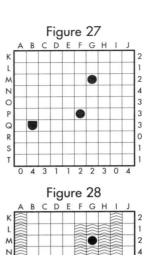

Figure 27

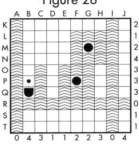

Figure 28

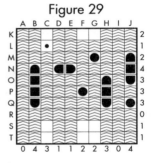

Figure 29

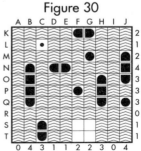

Figure 30

egy: Where can the biggest remaining ship go? In this case, you still need to place two destroyers. You can fit one of them in column C and the other in row K. They can't go anywhere else, so that's where they must be. The destroyer in row K must go at FK-GK, so CK is water, leaving CS-CT for the other destroyer (Figure 30).

From here, you just need to make the dot at CL a submarine and fill the blank squares with water, and you're done (Figure 31).

It's time for a toughie (Figure 32).

By now, the basic strategies should be second nature to you; applying them, your grid should look like Figure 33.

Now you'll need some deep thought. Where can the battleship go? Only in row M or row N. But you can be even more specific than that. It can't go at BM-CM-DM-EM because then AN, BN, CN, DN, EN, and FN would contain water, not leaving enough spaces for four ship segments in row N. Similarly, it can't go at BN-CN-DN-EN, because then row M would be impossible. So either the battleship goes at ABCD in one of these rows (M or N) with F and HIJ occupied in the other *or* it goes at CDEF in one of these rows with A and HIJ occupied in the other. In either case, the one at the bottom of column A is filled in row M or N, as is the one of column D and the one of column I. So you can put water in all the empty spaces in columns A, D, and I other than those in rows M and N (Figure 34).

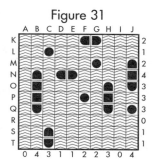

Figure 31

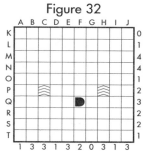

Figure 32

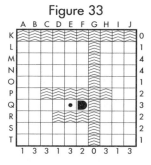

Figure 33

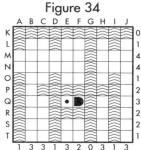

Figure 34

Back to the basic strategies—they'll bring you to Figure 35.

You already know the battleship and one of the cruisers will go somewhere in rows M and N. Where will the other cruiser go? The only possibility is column B. Row Q and column E can be ruled out for obvious reasons. Columns C, H, and J are out because, as discussed above, at least one square in each of those columns will be part of a horizontal ship in row M or N. The cruiser in column B will account for all three hits in the column, so the battleship must go at CDEF of either row M or N, and either AM or AN must be a submarine. You can now place the cruiser in column B. Since it must include BP, its top is at BN, BO, or BP. If it were at BN or BO, then both AN and CN would contain water, making rows M and N impossible to finish, so the top of the cruiser must be at BP. Placing the cruiser at BP-BQ-BR and—of course—applying the basic strategies, yields Figure 36.

Now look at column C. Three of those four squares must have ship segments. The battleship fits horizontally into either row M or N, taking up one of those three spaces. If it went in row M, then CL and CN would both contain water, making column C impossible. So the battleship goes at CN-DN-EN-FN. With basic strategies, you'll get Figure 37.

Check out the submarines—they've all been placed. That means the dot at JP can't be

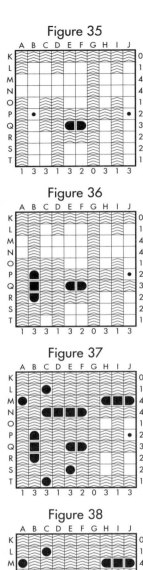

Figure 35

Figure 36

Figure 37

Figure 38

a submarine, so it must be part of a destroyer. And that gives you enough information to finish the puzzle (Figure 38).

One more puzzle (Figure 39) and then you're on your own to discover new, more advanced strategies.

Basic strategies doesn't help much (Figure 40).

Our advanced strategies don't help much either. The battleship can go in a number of places, and none of the rows or columns are within one of being filled. What can you do? Sometimes solving the really hard puzzle requires trial and error. You just have to take a guess, and if it doesn't work, you have to take another.

The battleship can go in two places in column G and in six places in column I. Try them until one works. As soon as one works you can stop, because all Battleships have unique answers. Try the first of two locations in column G, namely GP-GQ-GR-GS. After surrounding the battleship with water, and completing column G with water, the next step is to complete col-

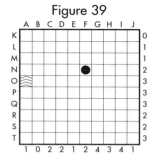

Figure 39

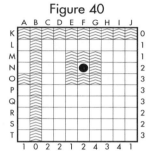

Figure 40

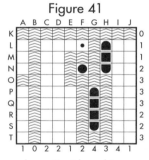

Figure 41

umn H with a cruiser at HL-HM-HN and complete column F with a ship segment at LF. But wait! Now row L has two ship segments (Figure 41), which is one too many, so the battleship doesn't go at GP-GQ-GR-GS. (If you went ahead and did basic strategies, you may have reached an impossible situation elsewhere in the grid.)

Moving on, try the battleship at the bottom of column G. Surround the ship with water and complete column F with a ship segment at FL and complete column G with water at GL. Now look at row L. Make the ship segment a submarine and complete the row with water. Now complete column H with a cruiser at HM-HN-HO and surround it with water. This leaves column I with four consecutive spaces that need to be filled, but the battleship can't go there since it's already in column G (Figure 42).

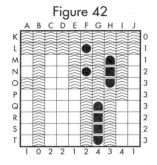

Figure 42

You now know the battleship is in column I. Try placing it next to the top, at IL-IM-IN-IO. (It can't start at IK since row K has no ship segments.) Surround the ship with water, and complete column I with water. Complete rows L, M, and N with water, and complete row O with a destroyer at CO-DO. Fill in the water surrounding the destroyer and complete row P with a submarine at AP and a destroyer at FP-GP. Surround that destroyer with water, and complete columns A and F with water. Now row Q must have a destroyer at CQ-DQ and a submarine at JQ. Surround the destroyer with water and complete columns C, D, and J with water. At last, there is an impossibility. Row R must have another destroyer in it, but there are none left. Also, columns G and H must both have cruisers in them adjacent to each other (Figure 43).

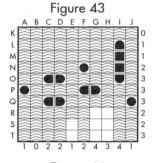

Figure 43

Onward you go, to IM-IN-IO-IP. Start by surrounding the battleship with water and completing its column with water. Next, complete column H with a cruiser at HR-HS-HT and surround it with water. This makes column G impossible (Figure 44).

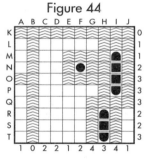

Figure 44

Next up is IN-IO-IP-IQ. Start by surrounding the battleship with water and completing its column with water. Next, complete column H with a submarine at HL and a destroyer at HS-HT. Complete row L with water and surround the destroyer with water and column G becomes impossible (Figure 45).

Just three more possibilities. At this point you may start worrying that none of these three will work and that you'll have to go back and redo everything you've done so far to find your mistake. That's the wrong way to think. Have confidence! Keep working.

Moving down one more spot yields IO-IP-IQ-IR. As usual, surround the battleship with water and complete its column with water. Then complete column H with a destroyer at HL-ML and a ship segment at HT. Complete rows L and M with water and fill in water at GS (since it's diagonally adjacent to HT). Complete column G with a cruiser at GP-GQ-GR and a ship segment at GT, and surround the cruiser with water. Row O can be completed with a destroyer at CO-DO, and the water surrounding it can be filled in. Now both AN and AP must have ship segments to complete rows N and P, but column A can only have one ship segment in it, so it's yet another impossibility (Figure 46).

The next possibility is IP-IQ-IR-IS. This one doesn't last long at all. After surrounding the battleship with water and completing its column, there's an impossibility in row O (Figure 47).

So you are left with only one possibility, namely IQ-IR-IS-IT. It had better work! Basic strategies don't take you too far (Figure 48).

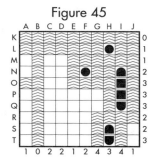

Figure 45

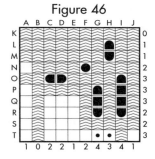

Figure 46

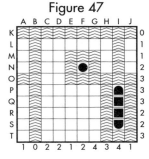

Figure 47

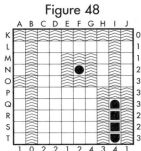

Figure 48

Don't be discouraged, though. You've made it this far. You'll sink this fleet yet! Move on to advanced strategy. Where can the longest not-yet-placed ship go? The cruisers can only go in column G, column H, or row P. If it went in row P though, row O would be impossible. Here's why: If the cruiser were at CP-DP-EP or at DP-EP-FP, then CO and DO would have to be water, leaving too few empty spaces in row O. If the cruiser were at EP-FP-GP, then DO and HO would have to be water, again leaving too few empty spaces in row O. Since those are the only three places where the cruiser can go in row P, it must not go there. That leaves you only two places for the two cruisers, so they must go in those places: columns G and H. You don't know exactly where, but you do know that GR must contain a ship segment, as well as both HM and HN (Figure 49).

Using basic strategies now, you get Figure 50.

Now, if GP were empty, then column G would need a battleship to fill it. But you've already used the battleship, so GP must have a ship segment. Similarly, GT can't be empty or else column G would need a battleship, so it too has a ship segment (Figure 51).

From here you can use basic strategies (starting off with water in HO since it's diagonally adjacent to GP, which has a ship segment in it) to finish up (Figure 52).

So there you have it. There are plenty of

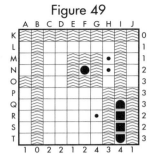

Figure 49

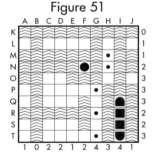

Figure 50

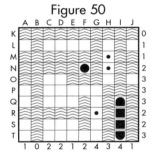

Figure 51

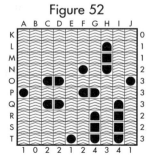

Figure 52

other strategies to use, depending on the puzzle. For example, if all the submarines are already in place, then every remaining ship segment must be a part of a longer ship, and if there's a column with a one that crosses a row with a one then it must contain water, since if it contained a ship, it would be a fifth submarine. Similarly, if three submarines are in place and there's a row with a two that has both adjacent rows filled with water, then you know the row with the two has to be a destroyer, not two submarines, since only one submarine is left to place. And then there's the case when ... well, you get the idea. Part of the fun is discovering new strategies.

And the best way to develop new strategies is to solve lots of puzzles. That's what lies ahead on the pages that follow. The puzzles are given six ranks, indicated on the right side of the right pages. From easiest to hardest, they are Seaman, Petty Officer, Ensign, Captain, Commodore, and Admiral. A salute and a tip of our cap to anyone who can solve all the Admiral puzzles. Good luck and ahoy!   —Peter Gordon & Mike Shenk

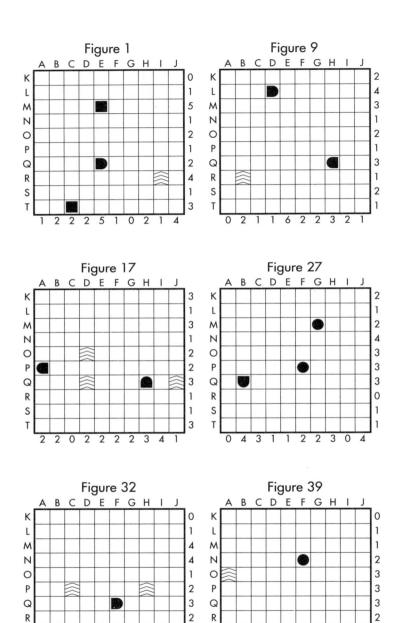

Figure 1

Figure 9

Figure 17

Figure 27

Figure 32

Figure 39

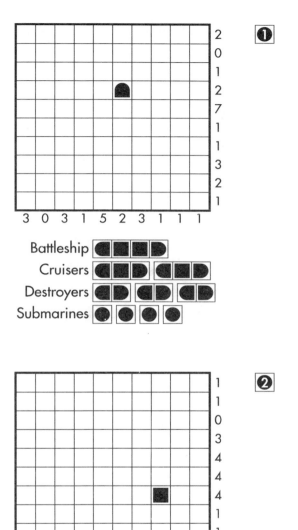

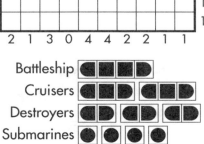

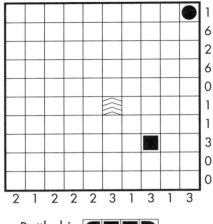

Battleship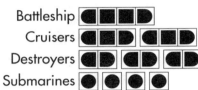

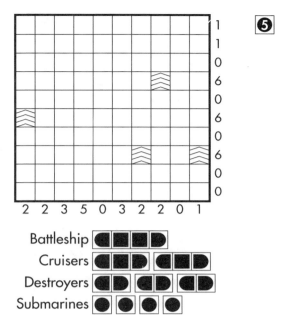

⑤

Battleship

Cruisers

Destroyers

Submarines

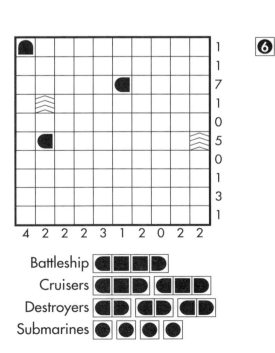

⑥

Battleship

Cruisers

Destroyers

Submarines

7

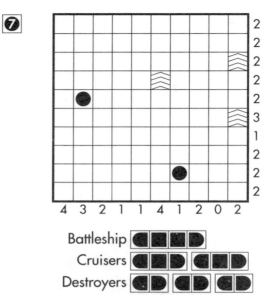

Battleship

Cruisers

Destroyers

Submarines

8

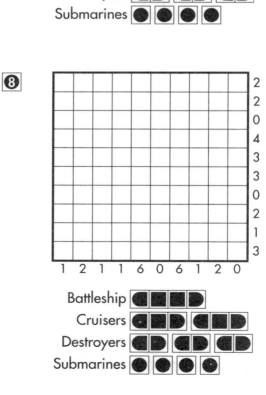

Battleship

Cruisers

Destroyers

Submarines

26

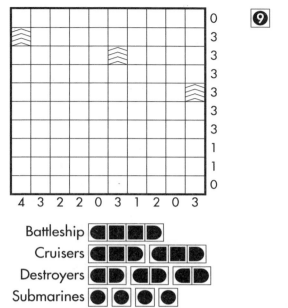

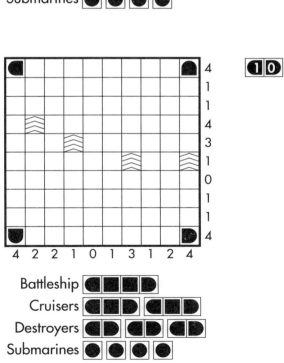

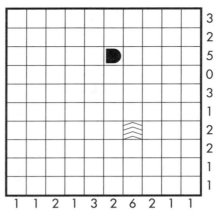

Column totals: 1 1 2 1 3 2 6 2 1 1

Row totals: 3 2 5 0 3 1 2 2 1 1

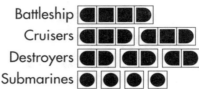

Battleship

Cruisers

Destroyers

Submarines

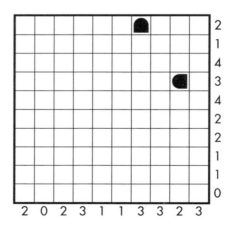

Column totals: 2 0 2 3 1 1 3 3 2 3

Row totals: 2 1 4 3 4 2 2 1 1 0

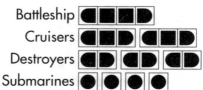

Battleship

Cruisers

Destroyers

Submarines

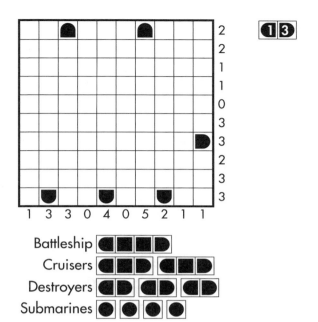

Battleship

Cruisers

Destroyers

Submarines

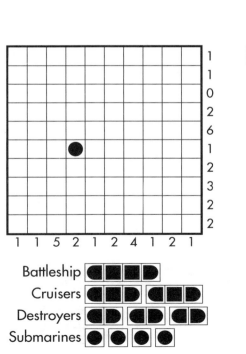

Battleship

Cruisers

Destroyers

Submarines

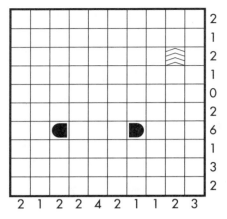

| 2 |
| 1 |
| 2 |
| 1 |
| 0 |
| 2 |
| 6 |
| 1 |
| 3 |
| 2 |

2 1 2 2 4 2 1 1 2 3

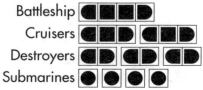

Battleship
Cruisers
Destroyers
Submarines

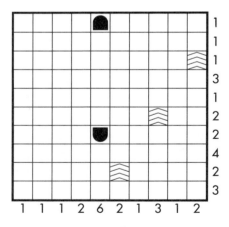

| 1 |
| 1 |
| 1 |
| 3 |
| 1 |
| 2 |
| 2 |
| 4 |
| 2 |
| 3 |

1 1 1 2 6 2 1 3 1 2

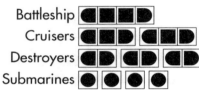

Battleship
Cruisers
Destroyers
Submarines

30

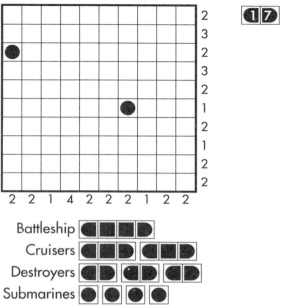

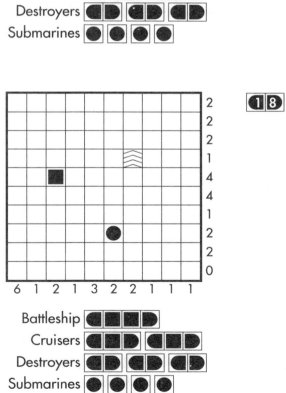

19

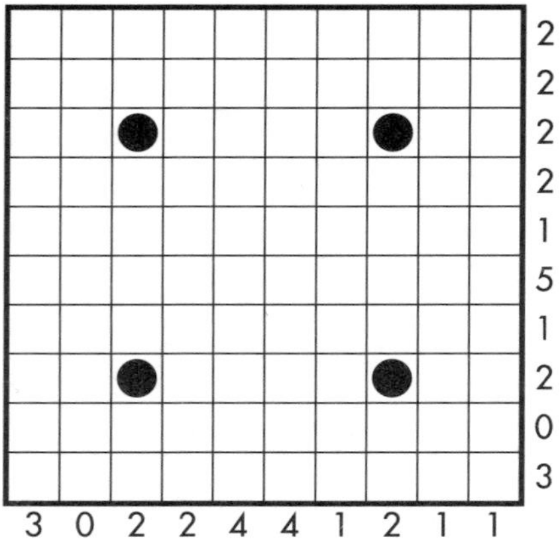
2
2
2
2
1
5
1
2
0
3
3 0 2 2 4 4 1 2 1 1

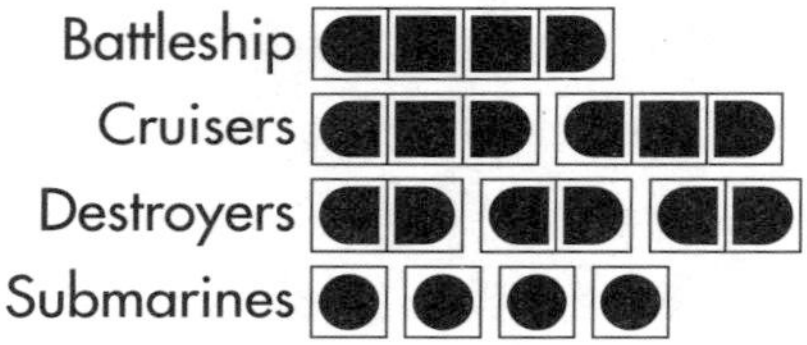
Battleship
Cruisers
Destroyers
Submarines

20

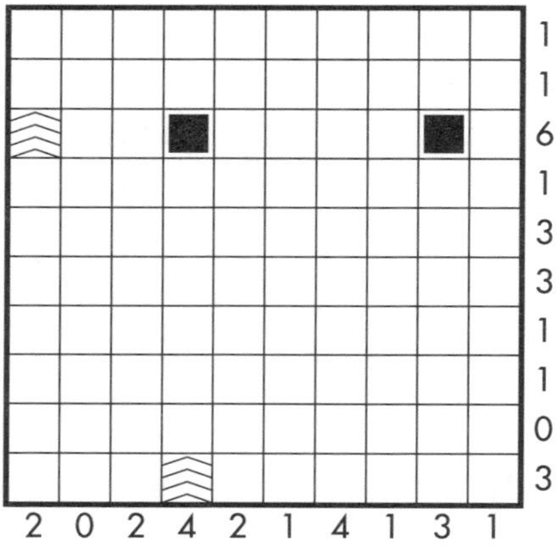
1
1
6
1
3
3
1
1
0
3
2 0 2 4 2 1 4 1 3 1

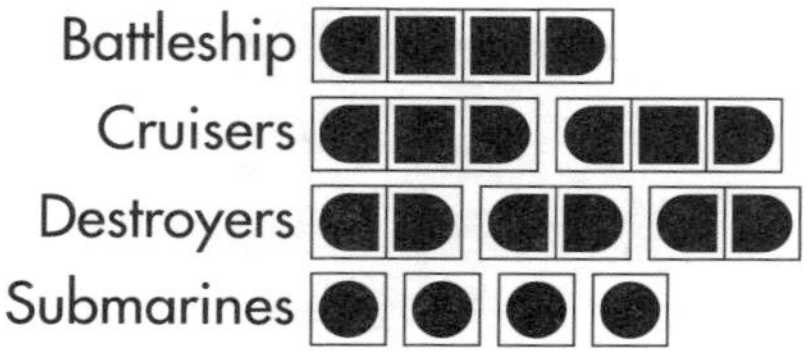
Battleship
Cruisers
Destroyers
Submarines

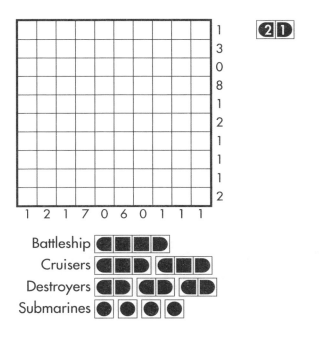

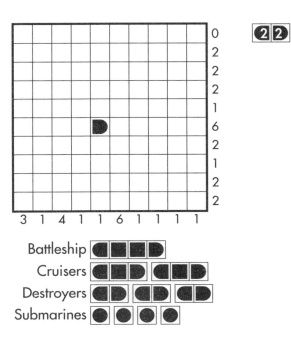

2 3

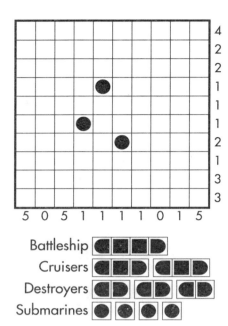

Battleship

Cruisers

Destroyers

Submarines

2 4

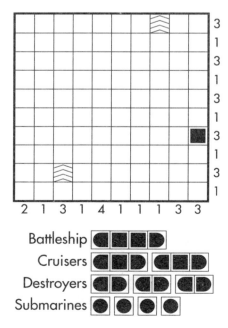

Battleship

Cruisers

Destroyers

Submarines

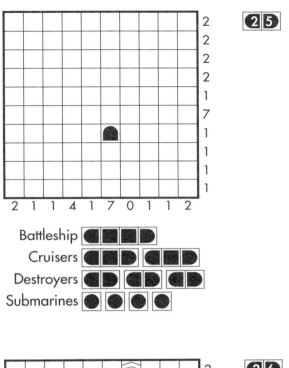

Battleship
Cruisers
Destroyers
Submarines

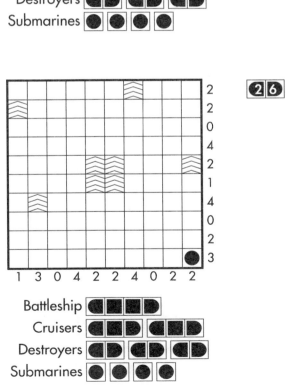

Battleship
Cruisers
Destroyers
Submarines

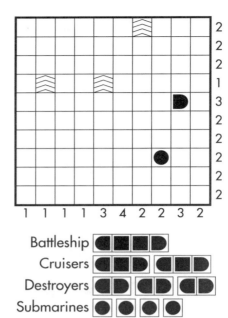

Battleship

Cruisers

Destroyers

Submarines

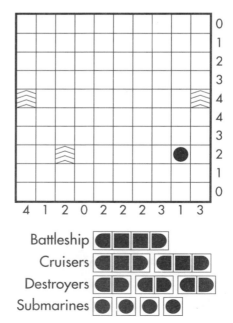

Battleship

Cruisers

Destroyers

Submarines

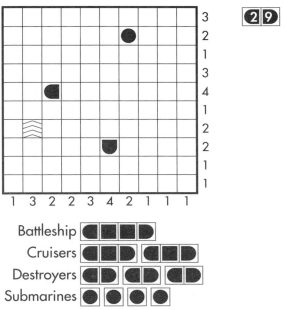

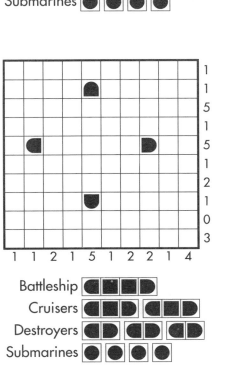

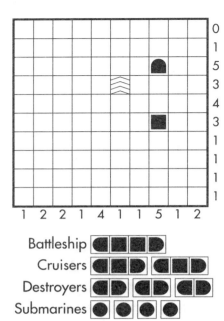

Battleship

Cruisers

Destroyers

Submarines

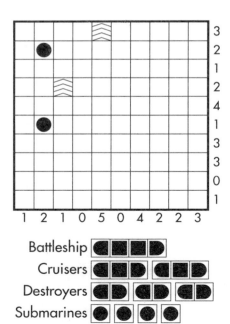

Battleship

Cruisers

Destroyers

Submarines

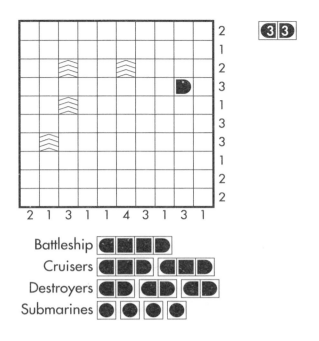

33

Battleship
Cruisers
Destroyers
Submarines

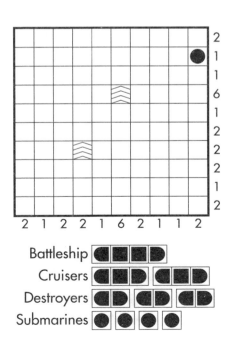

34

Battleship
Cruisers
Destroyers
Submarines

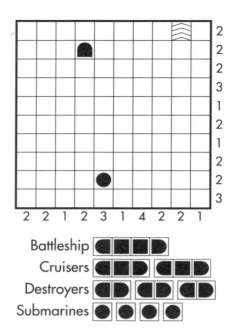

35

Battleship

Cruisers

Destroyers

Submarines

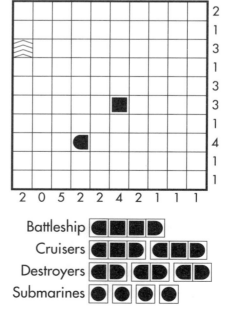

36

Battleship

Cruisers

Destroyers

Submarines

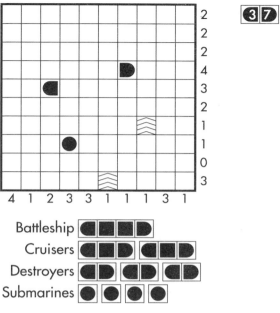

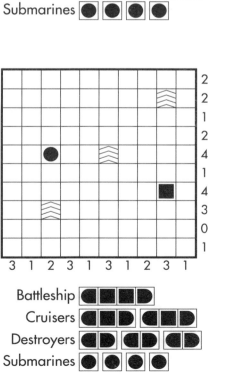

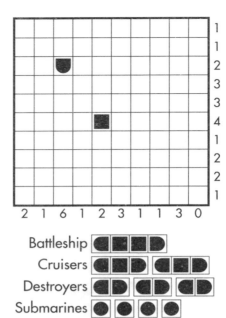

Battleship
Cruisers
Destroyers
Submarines

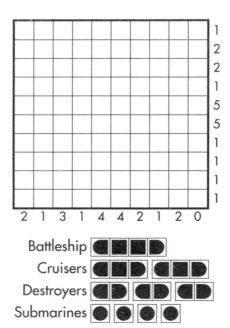

Battleship
Cruisers
Destroyers
Submarines

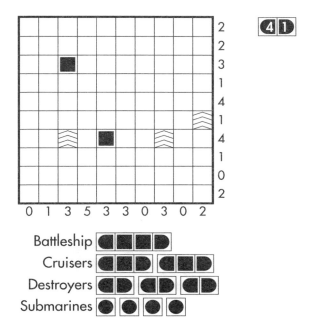

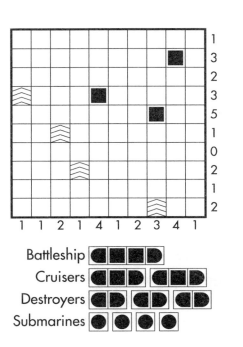

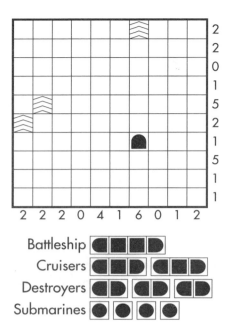

Battleship
Cruisers
Destroyers
Submarines

4 4

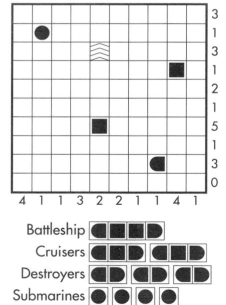

Battleship
Cruisers
Destroyers
Submarines

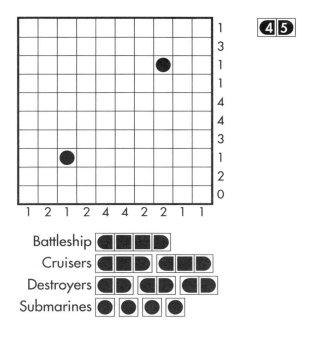

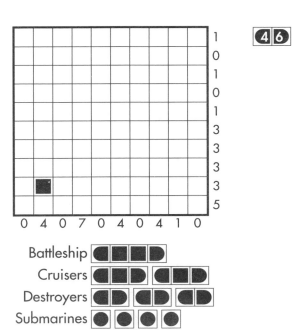

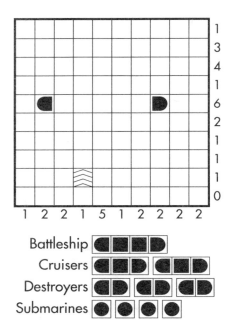

Battleship

Cruisers

Destroyers

Submarines

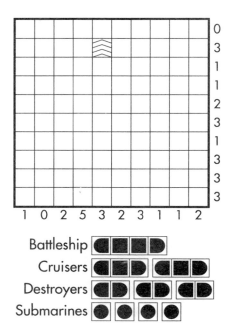

Battleship

Cruisers

Destroyers

Submarines

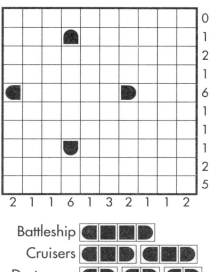

2	1	1	6	1	3	2	1	1	2

0
1
2
1
6
1
1
1
1
2
5

Battleship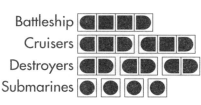
Cruisers
Destroyers
Submarines

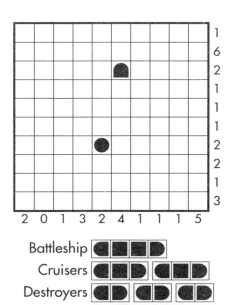

| 2 | 0 | 1 | 3 | 2 | 4 | 1 | 1 | 1 | 5 |

1
6
2
1
1
1
2
2
1
3

Battleship
Cruisers
Destroyers
Submarines

5 1

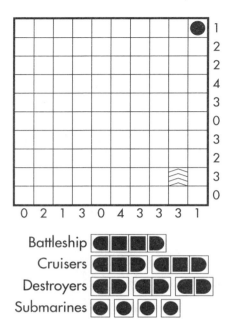

Battleship

Cruisers

Destroyers

Submarines

5 2

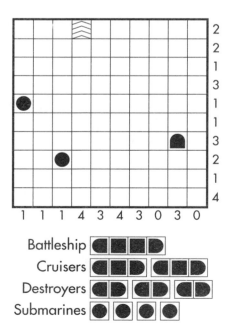

Battleship

Cruisers

Destroyers

Submarines

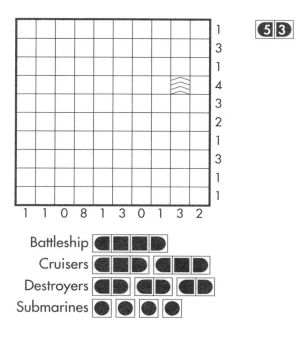

53

Battleship
Cruisers
Destroyers
Submarines

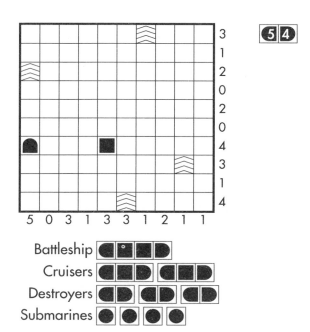

54

Battleship
Cruisers
Destroyers
Submarines

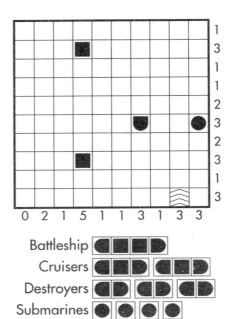

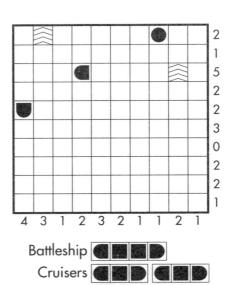

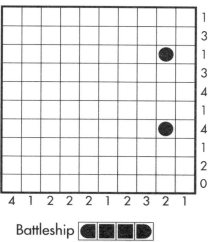

Battleship
Cruisers
Destroyers
Submarines

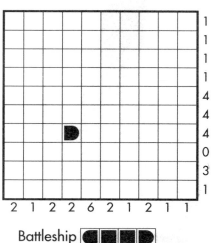

Battleship
Cruisers
Destroyers
Submarines

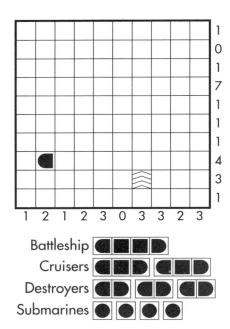

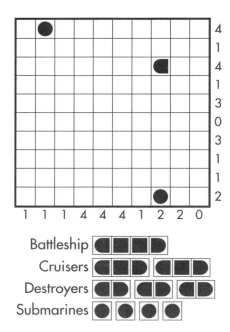

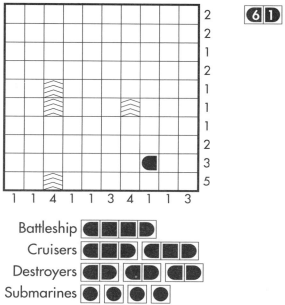

61

Battleship
Cruisers
Destroyers
Submarines

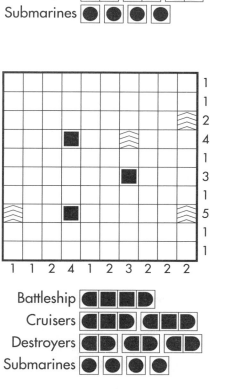

62

Battleship
Cruisers
Destroyers
Submarines

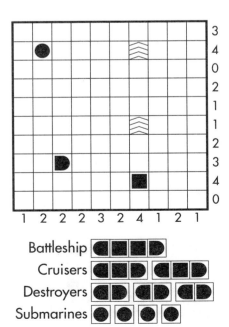

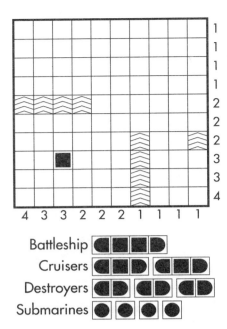

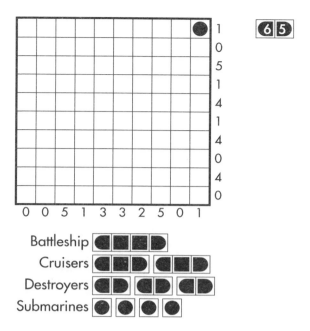

65

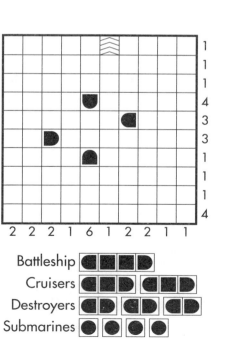

66

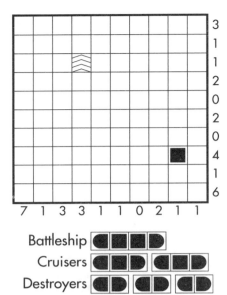

										3
										1
										1
										2
										0
										2
										0
										4
										1
										6

7 1 3 3 1 1 0 2 1 1

Battleship
Cruisers
Destroyers
Submarines

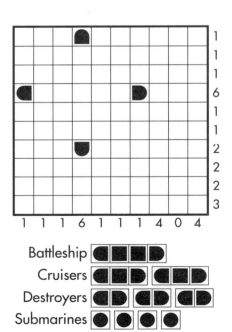

Battleship
Cruisers
Destroyers
Submarines

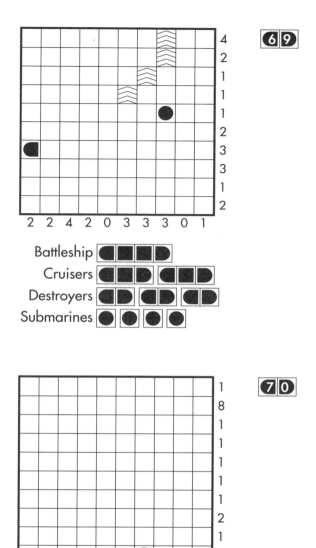

69

Battleship

Cruisers

Destroyers

Submarines

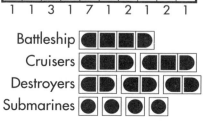

70

Battleship

Cruisers

Destroyers

Submarines

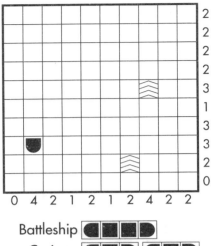

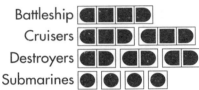

Battleship

Cruisers

Destroyers

Submarines

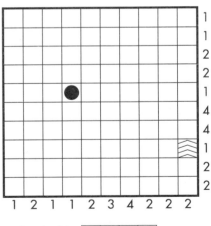

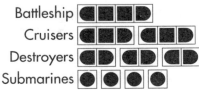

Battleship

Cruisers

Destroyers

Submarines

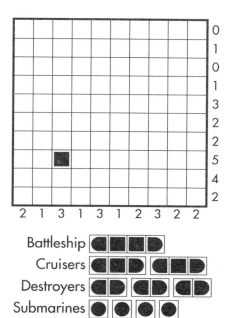

Battleship
Cruisers
Destroyers
Submarines

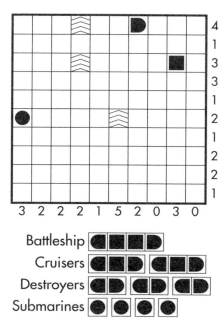

Battleship
Cruisers
Destroyers
Submarines

7 5

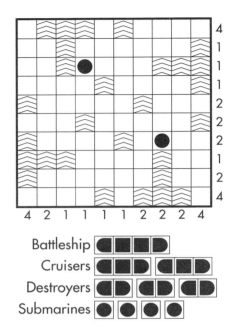

7 6

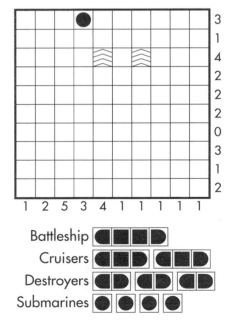

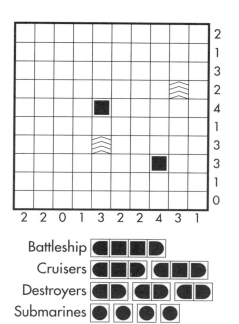

Battleship

Cruisers

Destroyers

Submarines

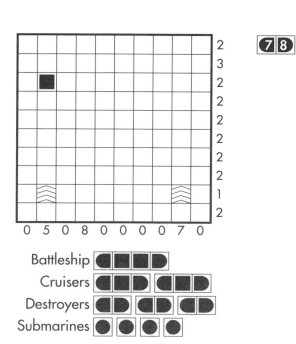

Battleship

Cruisers

Destroyers

Submarines

79

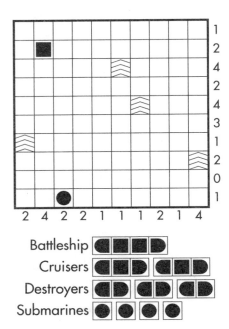

Battleship

Cruisers

Destroyers

Submarines

80

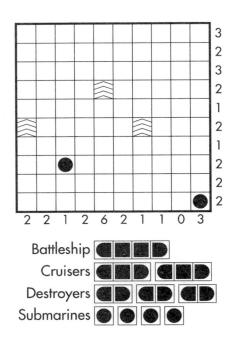

Battleship

Cruisers

Destroyers

Submarines

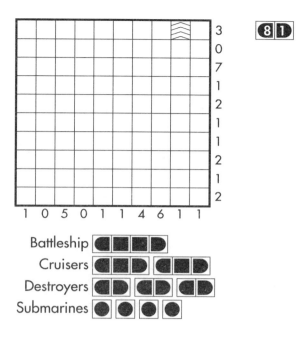

81

Battleship
Cruisers
Destroyers
Submarines

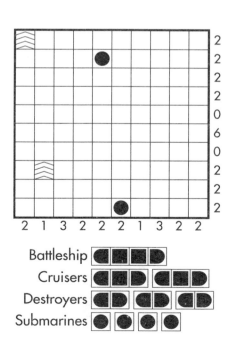

82

Battleship
Cruisers
Destroyers
Submarines

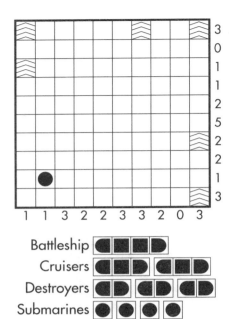

Battleship

Cruisers

Destroyers

Submarines

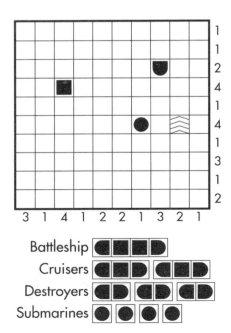

Battleship

Cruisers

Destroyers

Submarines

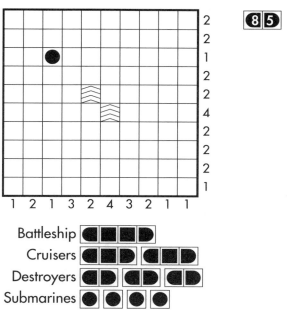

Battleship

Cruisers

Destroyers

Submarines

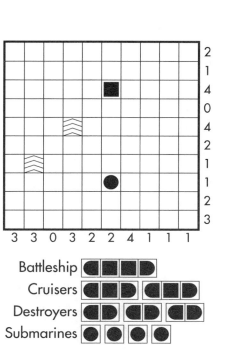

Battleship

Cruisers

Destroyers

Submarines

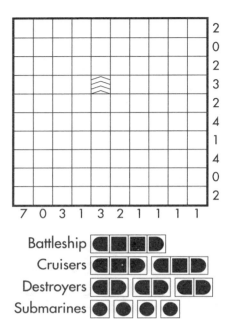

Battleship

Cruisers

Destroyers

Submarines

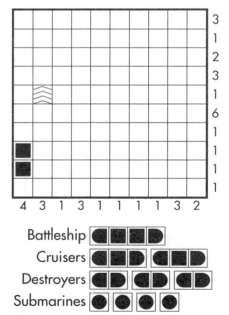

Battleship

Cruisers

Destroyers

Submarines

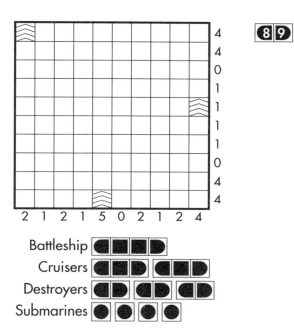

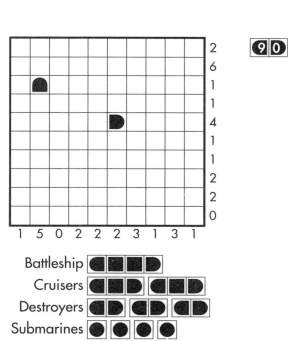

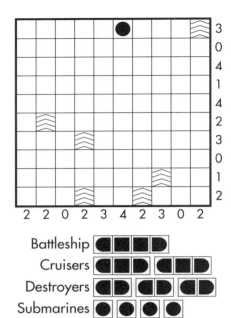

3
0
4
1
4
2
3
0
1
2

2 2 0 2 3 4 2 3 0 2

Battleship
Cruisers
Destroyers
Submarines

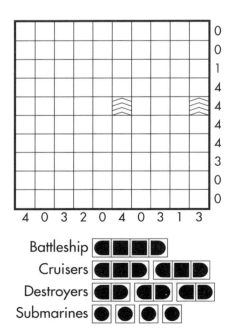

0
0
1
4
4
4
4
3
0
0

4 0 3 2 0 4 0 3 1 3

Battleship
Cruisers
Destroyers
Submarines

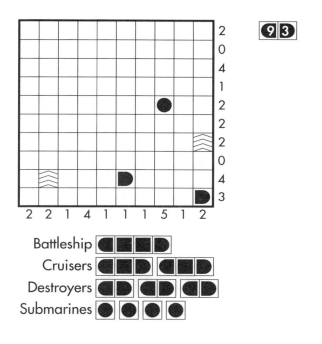

Battleship
Cruisers
Destroyers
Submarines

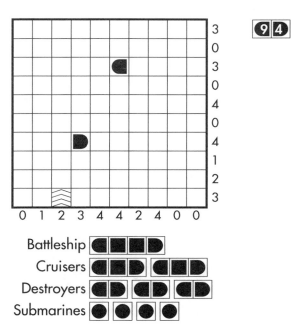

Battleship
Cruisers
Destroyers
Submarines

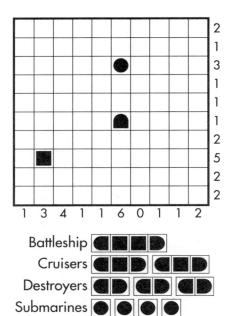

Battleship
Cruisers
Destroyers
Submarines

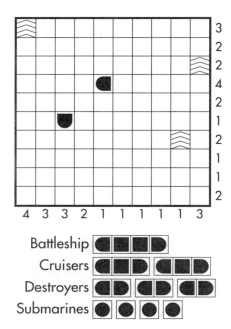

Battleship
Cruisers
Destroyers
Submarines

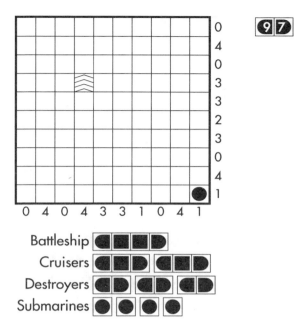

Battleship
Cruisers
Destroyers
Submarines

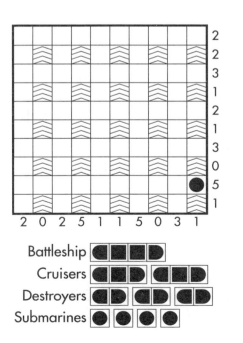

Battleship
Cruisers
Destroyers
Submarines

Admiral

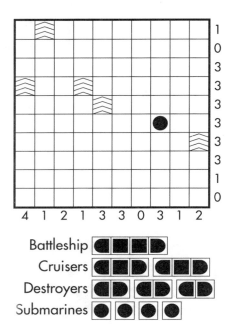

Battleship
Cruisers
Destroyers
Submarines

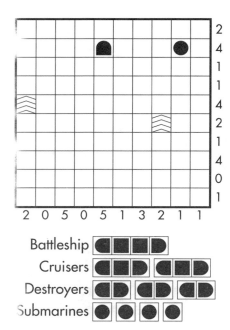

Battleship
Cruisers
Destroyers
Submarines

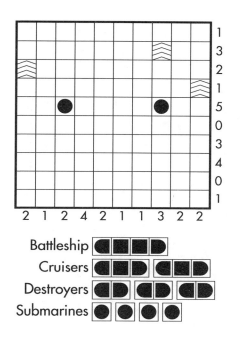

101

Battleship

Cruisers

Destroyers

Submarines

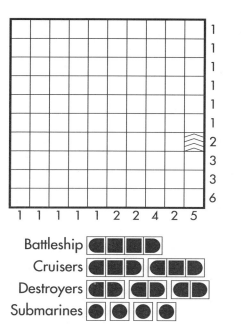

102

Battleship

Cruisers

Destroyers

Submarines

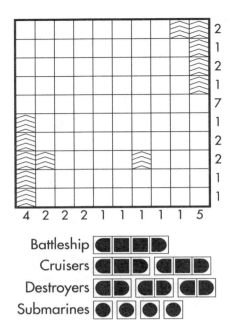

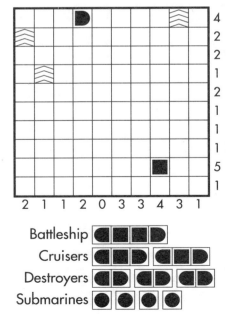

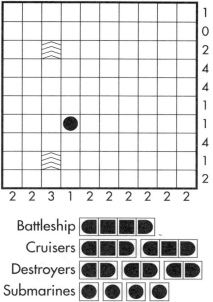

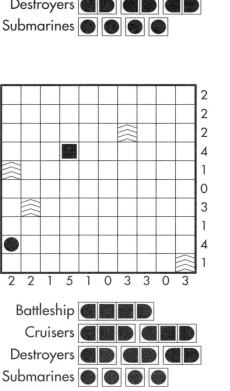

Admiral

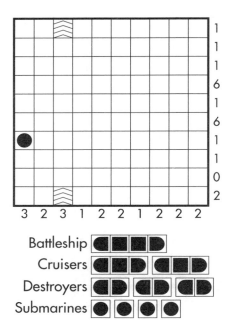

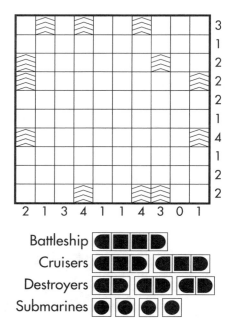

76

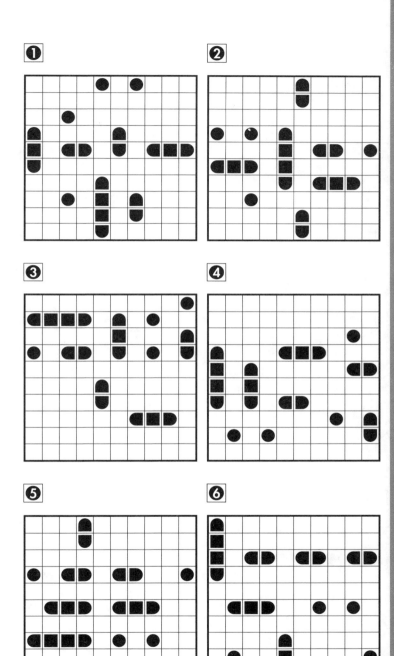

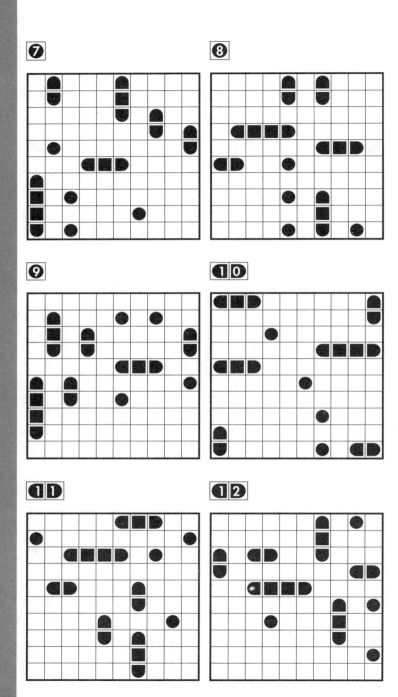

13

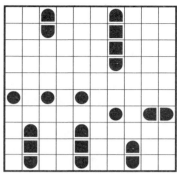

14

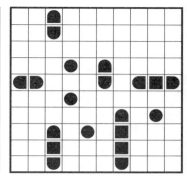

15

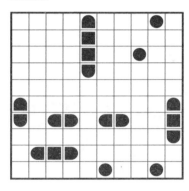

16

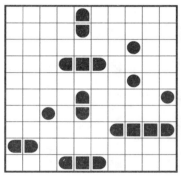

17

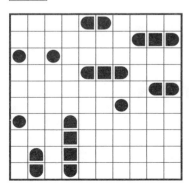

18

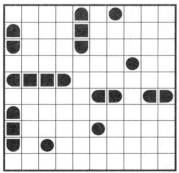

 Answers

 79

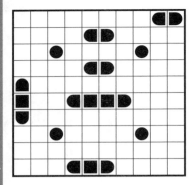

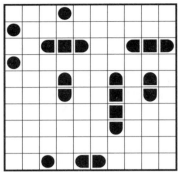

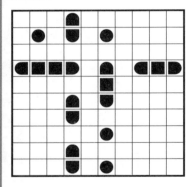

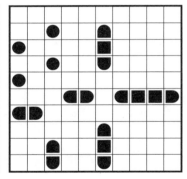

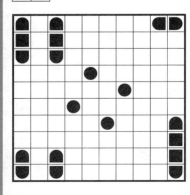

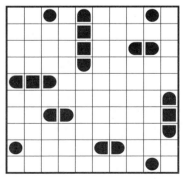

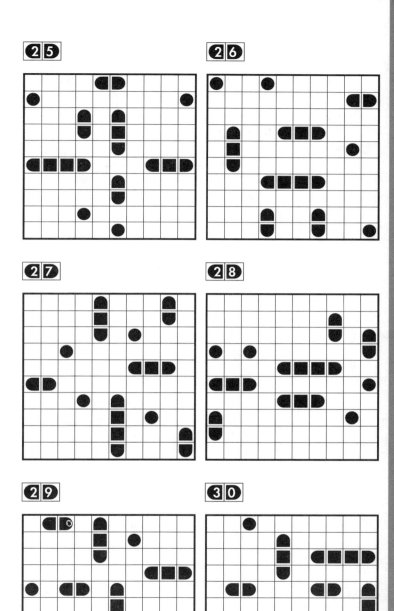

3 1

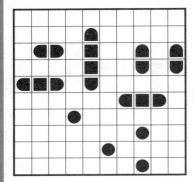

3 2

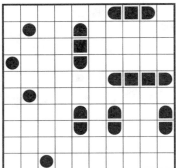

3 3

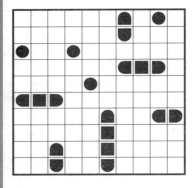

3 4

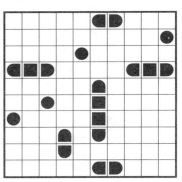

3 5

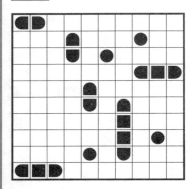

3 6

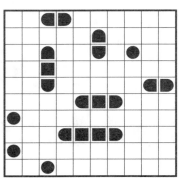

37

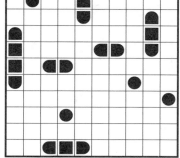

38

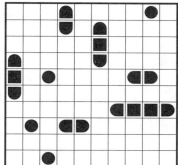

39

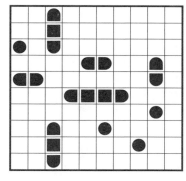

40

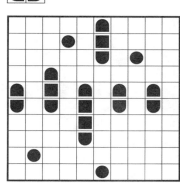

41

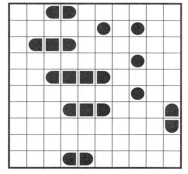

42

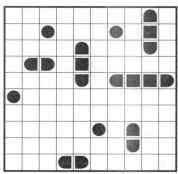

43

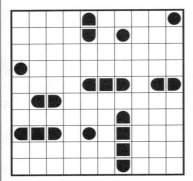

44

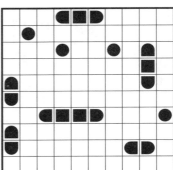

45

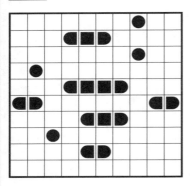

46

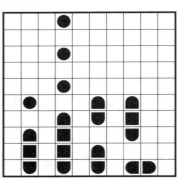

47

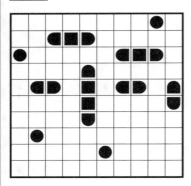

48

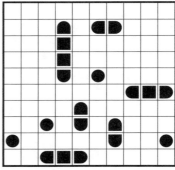

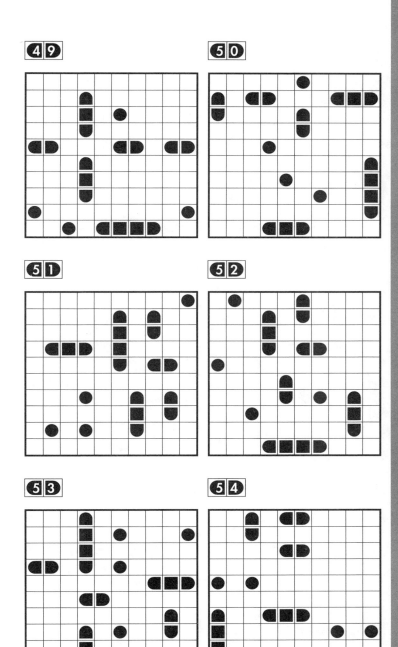

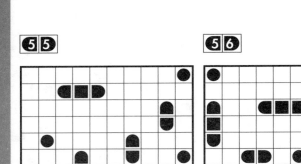

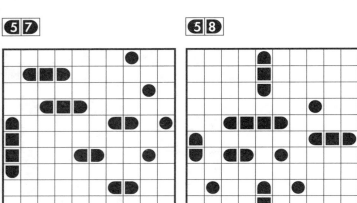

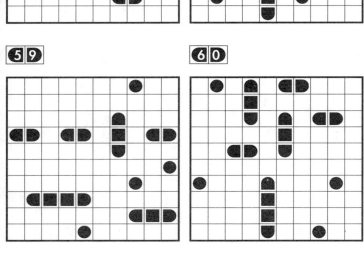

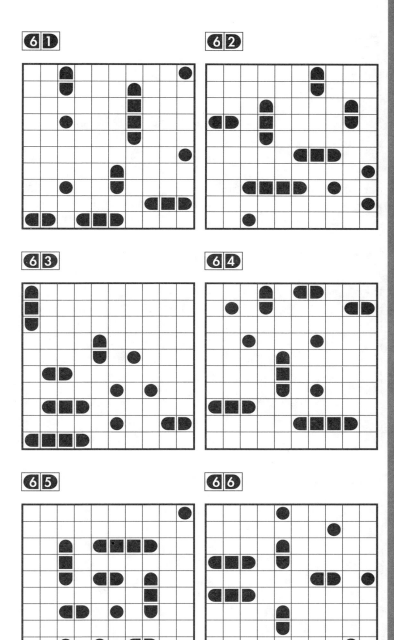

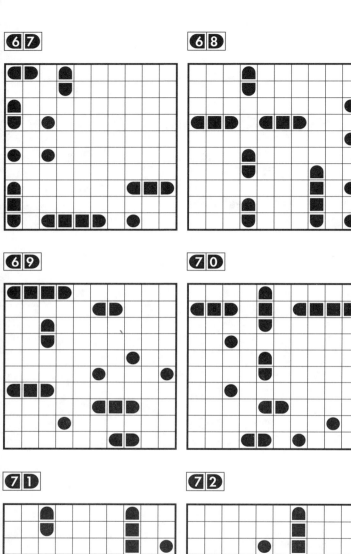

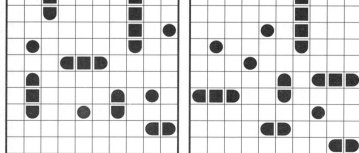

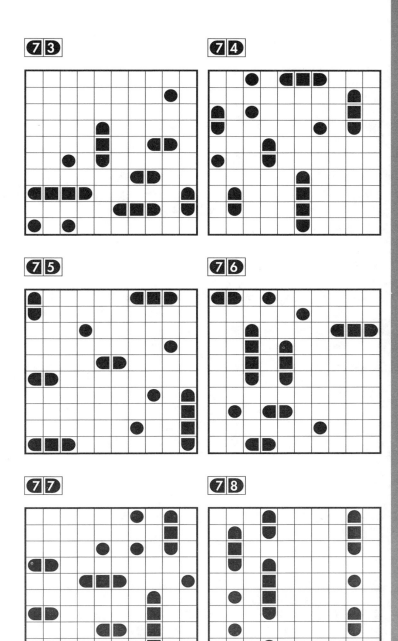

79 **80**

81 **82**

83 **84**

85

86

87

88

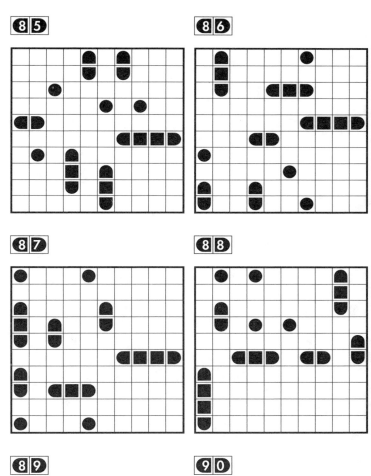

89

90

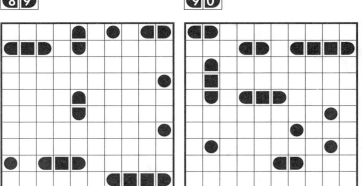

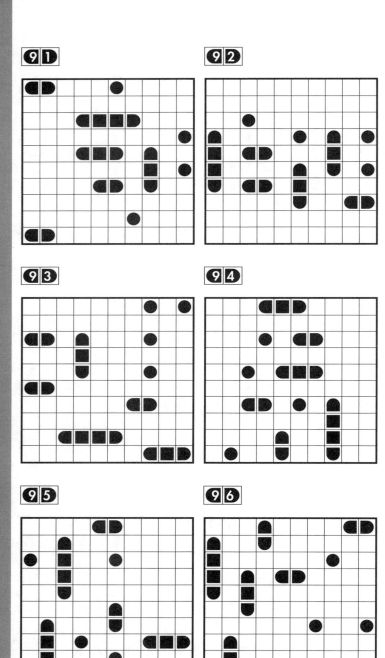

97

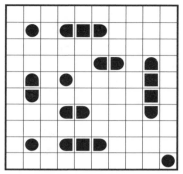

98

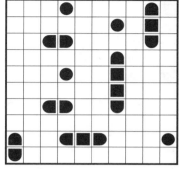

99

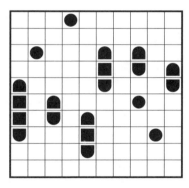

100

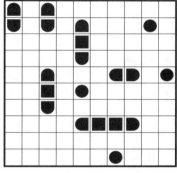

101

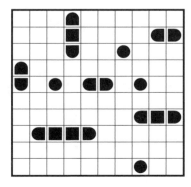

102

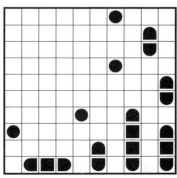

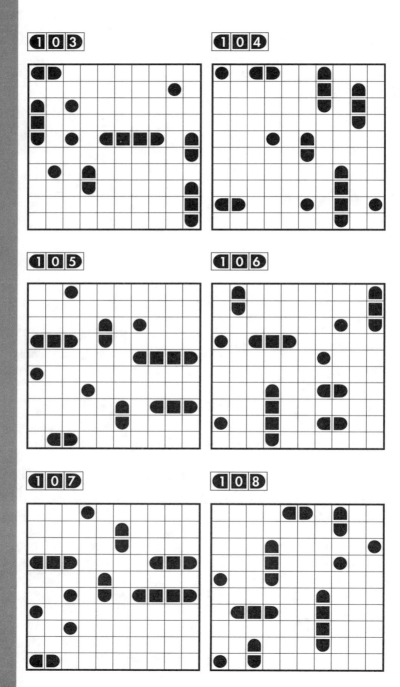

INDEX

Answer pages are in boldface

ABOUT THE AUTHORS

PETER GORDON is a puzzle editor and writer who lives in New York City. His crossword puzzles have appeared in numerous books, newspapers, and magazines, including *The New York Times*, *TV Guide*, and *Games Magazine*, where he was an editor for seven years. He enjoys traveling and deltiology (the hobby of collecting postcards).

MIKE SHENK, who also lives in New York City, is the crossword editor of *The Wall Street Journal*. He was an editor at *Games Magazine* for 16 years and is currently part of an on-line puzzle-consulting company called Puzzability. His puzzles appear regularly in *The New York Times*, *The New Yorker*, and at the annual American Crossword Puzzle Tournament.